EXCITING TITLES FROM Scobre EDUCATION

Contemporary Fiction & Sports Adventures

TALES OF THE UNCOOL
6-Book Series

These are the stories of the nerds, geeks, and freaks of Halsey Middle School — and how six self-proclaimed 'uncool' tweens took over their school.

Grades: 4-6
Ages: 8-12   Paperbacks: $8.99
Pages: 64   Library Bound: $27.99

MAGIC LOCKER ADVENTURES
6-Book Series

Three young friends find a magic locker, which takes them back in time. Historic sporting events are in jeopardy unless they right history!

Grades: 3-5
Ages: 8-11   Paperbacks: $8.99
Pages: 48   Library Bound: $27.99

ON THE HARDWOOD 30-Book Series

MVP Books invites readers to stand alongside their favorite NBA superstars *On the Hardwood*. These officially licensed NBA team bios provide an exciting opportunity to learn about where a team has been, and where they are going...

Grades: 4-6
Ages: 8-12   Paperbacks: $8.99
Pages: 48   Library Bound: $27.99

Common Core Aligned

 twitter.com/bookbuddymedia   facebook.com/bookbuddymedia

ORDER NOW!

Contact Lerner Publisher Services:
www.LernerBooks.com
Call: 800-328-4929   •   **Fax:** 800-332-1132

Lerner
PUBLISHER SERVICES

LITTLE LEAGUE
WORLD SERIES

BY SEAN JOHNSON

World's Greatest Sporting Events: Little League World Series

Copyright © 2015

Published by Scobre Educational

Written by Sean Johnson

Scobre Educational
2255 Calle Clara
La Jolla, CA 92037

Scobre Operations & Administration
42982 Osgood Road
Fremont, CA 94539

www.scobre.com
info@scobre.com

Scobre Educational publications may be purchased for educational, business, or sales promotional use.

Cover and layout design by Jana Ramsay
Edited by Zach Wyner
Copyedited by Renae Reed
Some photos by Newscom

ISBN: 978-1-62920-155-9 (Soft Cover)
ISBN: 978-1-62920-154-2 (Library Bound)
ISBN: 978-1-62920-153-5 (eBook)

INDEX

INTRODUCTION

Once considered America's "National **Pastime**," the sport of baseball has found a home the world over. From Tokyo, Japan to San Juan, Puerto Rico to Des Moines, Iowa, the game enjoys incredible popularity amongst people of all genders, ages and nationalities. However, nowhere is baseball more alive than in the imagination of the young. Children fantasize about making the big catch, throwing the final strike or crushing the game-winning home run for their favorite Major League team. All over the world, children dream of baseball, and every year, in the town of South Williamsport, Pennsylvania, a select group of children play out their dreams in real life.

The Little League World Series gives young boys and girls a massive stage to become legends of sport at the tender age of 12. While the

The Lincoln, Rhode Island team huddles before the beginning of a regional final.

road to this stage is long and tough, once these kids have arrived, they play nationally televised games before crowds that number in the thousands. Some wonder, why is the Little League World Series so popular? The answer is obvious. These kids are not professionals and they are not being paid to be there. They are children, who are more concerned with having fun than with making money, and the love of the game lights up their faces. The Little League World Series lifts the spirits of its participants and its millions of viewers. And the memories that these kids take with them become cherished possessions.

Hurler Jordan Brewer of Conejo Valley, California, pitching in the 2004 Little League World Series.

A LOOK BACK

Little League baseball dates all the way back to the late 1930s, a difficult time in U.S. and world history. The Stock Market Crash of 1929 and a terrible drought had plunged the United States into the Great Depression—an era in which a quarter of the American population could not find work and many lived in poverty. For a decade, working people around the world suffered. They hungered for more than food; they hungered for relief from worry.

In 1938, in South Williamsport, Pennsylvania, a man named Carl Stotz began organizing

young ballplayers on the local **sandlot**. Within a year, three teams—Lycoming Dairy, Jumbo Pretzel and Lundy Lumber—were formed. Right from the beginning, these games brought joy into the lives of local residents young and old. While baseball didn't fill anyone's bellies, it eased worries and soothed souls.

All the fun came to a grinding halt when Japanese aircraft

In the 1930s Little League baseball changed the lives of young boys in and around South Williamsport, Pennsylvania.

The sandlot in Williamsport was closed to the public during World War II.

bombed Pearl Harbor on December 6, 1941. In response to the attack, the United States joined the allied forces in World War II. Many Americans were sent overseas to fight. The young men and women that stayed home became part of the war effort, building ships, planes and weaponry. Open spaces were converted into factories. The sandlot in South Williamsport, Pennsylvania, that had been Little League baseball's original home, was taken over for war production.

Four years later, the war ended. While the United States still suffered from racism and inequality, joblessness and poverty were on the decline. After years of war, people looked for ways to forget their troubles and enjoy life. Little League baseball was a major step

People across the world came out en masse to celebrate the end of World War II.

in that direction.

In 1946, the league grew to 12 teams. A year later, that number erupted. Seventeen different leagues, each consisting of many teams, competed against one another. With so much competition, Little League baseball decided to create a Little League World Series that would give the best teams from each region a chance to compete for a championship.

In the **inaugural** Little League World Series, the hometown team from South Williamsport, Pennsylvania defeated the Lock Haven All Stars, 16-7. The tournament was a success.

Here was the beautiful game of baseball being played with joy, wonder, imagination and equality. While Jackie Robinson was just integrating Major League baseball, Little League baseball had no restrictions based on race. On the Little League baseball diamond, all young boys were equal. The one thing they lacked was girl ballplayers. Unfortunately, it would take 30 years for that mistake to be corrected.

Of course, a team can't honestly call itself a "World Series Champion" unless it competes against teams from all over the world. In 1951, the first permanent Little League outside of the United States was established in Canada. Then, after being broadcast on national

West Tokyo brought home Japan's first Little League World Series championship in 1967.

Girls became official Little League World Series participants in the early 1970s.

television, Little League baseball went global. Over the course of a decade, teams from Venezuela, Spain, Chinese Taipei, Berlin and Japan all joined in the fun. With the inclusion of teams from Japan and Germany, Little League baseball provided the world an opportunity to heal, as the children and grandchildren of former enemies engaged in friendly competition.

Little League baseball took another giant step forward in 1972 after the passage of Title IX—an amendment to the Higher Education Act that outlawed exclusion based on gender. That year, 12-year-old Maria Pepe pitched three Little League games for the Young Democrats of Hoboken, New Jersey. Recognizing that the time was long overdue for girls to join the party, Little League baseball officially created a league for girls in 1974.

Today, Little League baseball has grown to previously unimaginable levels. The Little League World Series features 16 teams (eight American and eight **international**).

The Apopka, Florida catcher can't hide his displeasure as Japan scores the game-winning run.

The United States Champion plays the International Champion in the World Series Championship Game. All told, more than 2.3 million young ballplayers compete for the ultimate prize. Out of those millions of young ballplayers, about a dozen realize their dreams and become World Series Champions. But for every heartbreaking loss, the Little League World Series inspires countless fans and fantasies.

TIMELINE

1960 ●
Berlin, Germany becomes the first European team in the league. The league expands to host more than 5,500 leagues and the World Series Championship is broadcast for the first time live on ABC.

1940 — **1950** — **1960** — **1970**

1947 ●
The inaugural National Little League Tournament is played in South Williamsport. The Maynard Midgets defeat the Lock Haven All Stars, 16-7. The tournament is later renamed the Little League World Series.

1951
The league's popularity expands and a team from British Columbia, Canada becomes the first permanent international team. Little Leagues throughout the country grow in number to 776.

1967 ●
West Tokyo, Japan becomes the first international team from the Far East to win the league title. Future Major League ballplayer Bobby Mitchell plays for Northridge Little League in the World Series.

1950 ●
Posing as a boy nicknamed "Tubby," Kathryn Johnston plays for the Kings Dairy Little League—the first girl to do so. For the next several years the "Tubby Rule" bars girls from playing in the league.

1971
The **aluminum bat** is introduced into Little League play. Future Major Leaguer Lloyd McClendon sets a Little League record, slugging five home runs in five at-bats and leading his team from Gary, Indiana to the Championship Game against Tainan, Taiwan.

1974

Following a lawsuit by Jenny Fulle, Little League rules are finally changed and girls are allowed to participate. Little League expands its programs to include softball leagues for both boys and girls.

2010

Game play is changed as the World Series eliminates pool play and incorporates **double-elimination**. A new division of Little League launches for 12- to 13-year-olds called the "50/70 program" in which the **pitcher's mound** is placed 50 feet from home plate and the distance between bases increases to 70 feet.

1992

Carl Stotz, founder of Little League baseball, dies.

| 1980 | 1990 | 2000 | 2010 |

1984

The first South Korean team from Seoul wins the championship, defeating the Altamonte Springs League of Florida. Belgium's Victoria Roche becomes the first girl to play in the Little League World Series.

2001

Following the completion of the Little League Volunteer Stadium in 2000, the Little League World Series expands. New rules allow eight U.S. and eight international teams to play in the tournament.

THE FUTURE

With players of different ages, genders and nationalities playing World Series softball and baseball, the size of the competition and the level of play continue to grow. With the Little League World Series approaching its 70th birthday, the tournament shows no signs of slowing down.

EQUIPMENT

A first baseball glove is special. It's more than an ordinary piece of equipment–it's an extension of your body that feels like a part of you. After buying a glove, kids get to participate in the age-old ritual of breaking it in.

Ask any parent or grandparent how to break in a glove and they're sure to have no shortage of advice. The goal is to soften the leather and form a good pocket so the baseball won't pop out when you

catch a fly ball or a sharp line drive. With this in mind, most people suggest rubbing the glove with oil. Some will suggest that you pound it with a hammer. Others might even suggest that the child ask a parent to drive over the glove with their car. Nowadays, these more extreme steps aren't quite as important, as many gloves are broken in prior to purchase. That said, you can't catch the ball consistently without a good pocket, and the best

way to get a good pocket is to play a ton of catch. After buying a glove, head out to the yard or the nearest park and throw the ball around until the sun goes down.

Once that leather glove is good and broken in, it's time to get a good pair of cleats and (for the boys) an athletic supporter and cup for safety. When finding those perfect

A dirty jersey is one sign of a day well spent.

cleats, be sure to select rubber ones because steel spiked cleats can be dangerous and are not allowed in Little League play.

Teams provide a lot of the basic needed gear. Each team will be given catcher's gear, batting helmets, bats, team jerseys and team hats. Full lists of supplied gear and needed equipment can be obtained from the team's manager.

Fans pack the hillside beyond the outfield wall at Howard J. Lamade Stadium.

The main venue for the World Series is Howard J. Lamade Stadium. This field was built in 1959 and can hold up to 40,000 spectators. Lamade Stadium is two-thirds the size of the average Major League stadium, with the base paths measuring 60 feet apart and the pitcher's mound set 46 feet from the plate. In 2006, the league increased the distance from home plate to the outfield fence by 20 feet (from 205 feet to 225 feet) to reduce the number of home runs.

The steady growth of Little League baseball created the need to add another venue. As a result, a second field was built in 2001 and was named

Mexico battles Venezuela at Little League Volunteer Stadium.

Little League Volunteer Stadium. The addition of the second stadium made it possible for eight U.S. and eight international teams to compete for the championship.

South Willamsport, Pennsylvania has been the home of the Little League World Series since the first year of competition back in 1947. Throughout the off-season, Lamade Stadium and Volunteer Stadium are kept clean and prepped but remain empty. When the event begins in August, players, parents and spectators descend on South Williamsport, bringing passion, excitement and a welcome boost to the local economy.

RULES

There are many rules in the game of baseball, some of them more complex and less frequently enforced than others. However, for kids that have spent their childhood watching their favorite Major League team, Little League baseball doesn't contain many surprises. The same basic rules that govern a Major League baseball game are followed in Little League. Four balls earn the batter a walk, three strikes and you're out, and three outs end an inning. Rules such as force outs, **tagging up** and tie goes to runner are all identical to the pros, and managerial decisions, such as relieving a pitcher and **pinch hitting** for a batter, also look the same.

The differences that do exist in Little League baseball are there primarily to protect younger players from too much wear and tear on their young bodies. One such rule is the pitch count. Little League pitchers need time to rest their arms after a game. Consequently, 11- to 12-year-olds can throw a maximum of 85 pitches in a single day. After throwing 85 pitches, they must be given four full days of rest. Any time a pitcher

Umpires enforce the rules on the field at the Little League World Series.

Strict rules are enforced to prevent pitchers from injuring themselves.

throws between 21 and 35 pitches, an entire day of rest is required.

In addition, Little League games are shorter. A complete game is six innings instead of nine; however, extra innings are played if the game is tied. Hitters, looking to end a game with a walk-off home run, do have one major advantage over their professional counterparts—Little League baseball allows the use of more powerful aluminum bats.

THE ROAD TO...

Participation in Little League baseball is easy. Young boys and girls merely need to sign up for a team that represents the geographical region in which they live. Once they have been placed on a team, the heights they reach are up to them. Success in baseball, just like success in all walks of life, requires more than the desire to succeed. It requires the relentless pursuit of a goal. While some players may start out with more natural athletic ability than others, the players that dedicate themselves to improving are the ones that become stars. Still, it would be dishonest to say that playing in the Little League World Series doesn't require a little bit of luck. There are simply too many great young ballplayers out there to suggest that hard work and dedication alone will get them to the tournament.

At end of the regular season, coaches decide which players from their region have separated themselves from the herd. Those chosen few make up the All-Star team that represents their region in several tournaments. Depending on the size of the state, some teams may need to play more games in order to rise to the top. The winners of these regional tournaments move on to participate in the Little League World Series.

Chula Vista, California coaches give their kids a pep talk before the first inning of a World Series game against Japan.

Teammates gather at home plate to celebrate a big home run.

BEST PERFORMANCES

TODD FRAZIER, 1998

Todd Frazier played for the Toms River, New Jersey team that beat Kashima, Ibaraka, Japan to win the 1998 Little League World Series championship. Frazier went on to become the third baseman for the Cincinnati Reds.

Todd Frazier led off the 1998 Little League World Series Championship Game with a home run. It was an incredible opening to a memorable game, but it would not be the high point of Frazier's day. In a barnburner of a game that featured 11 home runs, Frazier went 4-4 with one **RBI** and three runs scored. However, it was not with his bat, but with his arm that Frazier went from star to legend. Taking the mound with the score knotted at 8, Frazier pitched a stellar two innings to close out the game and earn the win. When he struck out the final batter to secure a 12-9 victory, he was mobbed by his ecstatic teammates.

JURICKSON PROFAR, 2004-2005

A star infielder and pitcher, Jurickson Profar helped the Pabao Little League of Willemstad, Curacao advance to two straight Little League World Series Championship Games in 2004 and 2005. Five years after leading his team to the championship, he signed a contract with Major League Baseball's Texas Rangers.

Profar was the top statistical pitcher in the 2004 Little League World Series. He posted a 2-0 record with one save in 12.1 innings of work. In those 12.1 innings, he scattered six hits and allowed only one run, while striking out 19. At the plate, he batted .313 (5-for-16) with a double, five runs batted in, a run scored and only two strikeouts. In the 2004 Championship Game against Thousand Oaks, California, Profar launched a three-run home run that proved to be the difference in a 5-2 victory.

JESUS SAUCEDA, 2008

Jesus Sauceda of Mexico turned in one of the all-time greatest performances in Little League history in 2008. The 13-year-old pitcher starred with his arm and his bat, leading Mexico to a resounding win.

In the 2008 Little League World Series Championship Game, Jesus Sauceda was absolutely perfect. At the plate, he went 3-3 with six runs batted in and a **grand slam**. On the mound, he was even more impressive. Sauceda pitched a **perfect game**, allowing zero base runners and striking out all 12 batters he faced. The game was called after just four innings because of the "Mercy Rule," with Mexico beating Italy, 12-0. Sauceda's perfect game was the fifth in Little League World Series history.

MO'NE DAVIS, 2014

In the 2014 installment of the Little League World Series, a pitching sensation by the name of Mo'ne Davis captured the minds and imaginations of a nation. Davis, a right-handed power pitcher for the Taney Dragons, which represented the city of Philadelphia in the 68th edition of the event, tossed a shutout against Nashville. That fact was exceptional in itself yet when you consider that Davis became the first girl in Little League World Series history to accomplish such a feat, her two-hit, eight-strikeout performance gained even further recognition. When the tweets about Mo'ne started arriving from the likes of First Lady Michelle Obama, baseball All-Stars Mike Trout and Andrew McCutchen and even basketball star Kevin Durant, Davis' celebrity hit a different level altogether.

Though Davis' 70 miles per hour fastball wasn't quite as dominant in her next outing against the team from Las Vegas, her popularity was apparent as her encore was the most watched game in the history of the event. Davis topped off her crazy week in the summer of 2014 by becoming the first Little Leaguer to grace the cover of Sports Illustrated.

THE RECORD BOOK

The Hsi Nan Little League team from Taichung, Chinese Taipei holds the record for most World Series titles with 17. They also set the record for consecutive titles by winning five straight years from 1977 to 1981.

In the 1953 World Series, Birmingham, Alabama beat Schenectady, New York by a score of 1-0. The 1968 Championship Game between Japan and Richmond ended in a 1-0 victory for the champions from Japan, and in the 2002 Championship, Williamsport, Kentucky defeated Sendai, Japan by the same score.

Chin-Hsiung Hsieh holds the title for most home runs in a Little League World Series with seven. His Little League team from Taiwan beat the U.S. team from Rhode Island 7-1 in the 1996 World Series Championship Game.

Ashton White of California and Brian Smith of Montreal, Quebec sit atop the leaders' list with three stolen bases in a single World Series Championship Game.

Chula Vista, California represented the West Region in the 2009 World Series. The team had a record-breaking 72 hits during the tournament en route to becoming Little League World Series Champions.

In the 2002 tournament, Kentucky native Aaron Alvey pitched a total of 22 innings, allowing only six hits and striking out 44 batters. He carried Williamsport to a 1-0 win in the Championship Game, shutting out Sendai, Japan, and hitting the game's lone run.

THE FANS

A young fan perches atop her father's shoulders to gain a better view.

Over the years, the Little League World Series has developed new fans at a rapid rate. Every player who participates has a following of friends and family, and their excitement for this event only furthers the already deep fan base. The admission price to the games is evidence of this fact. Entrance into Little League World Series games is free. In addition to the thousands of fans in attendance, millions of viewers watch the event on television every year. In 2013, 3.9 million fans tuned into ABC to watch the Championship Game, the tournament's highest viewership in six years.

Fans of the Ocean View Little League team celebrate as their team brings home the title.

In addition to watching the games, fans participate in the action by collecting commemorative, limited edition pins made by both local businesses and Little League baseball. Each team that participates in the tournament gets their very own team pin. These souvenirs become the treasured mementos of players and fans alike.

IMPACT

One way to assess the Little League World Series' impact is to look at the number of participants who have gone on to make a career of baseball. Forty-two Little League World Series players (including stars such as Derek Bell, Gary Sheffield and Jason Varitek) have made it all the way to the Major Leagues. Another is to look at the thousands of fans that flock to South Williamsport, Pennsylvania every year, bringing with them a $20 million boost to the local economy. However, the most compelling number when measuring the tournament's impact is 4,000,000 – the number of viewers who watch the action live on network television.

The lightning speed with which Little Leagues spread across the country and the world is proof of its broad appeal. Playing Little League baseball is something that children desperately want to do and it's also something that parents are eager to encourage. One reason is because it offers ballplayers a chance at glory. But this event does more than create heroes; it instills the values of teamwork and good sportsmanship. It teaches young athletes how to win and lose with grace and dignity.

As long as there has been baseball, young boys and girls have dreamed of being world champions. The Little League World Series turns a spotlight on those young dreamers and asks them, why wait? Let's play ball.

The Ocean View Little League team doles out high fives to their supporters, following their 2011 Little League World Series championship.

GLOSSARY

aluminum bat: baseball bat made with aluminum as opposed to wood. Aluminum bats can hit the ball faster and farther than wooden bats.

double-elimination: is a type of elimination tournament in which a participant can no longer win the tournament's championship after having lost two games.

grand slam: a home run hit with all three bases occupied by baserunners ("bases loaded"), thereby scoring four runs—the most possible in one play.

inaugural: marking the beginning of an institution, activity or period of office.

international: existing, occurring or carried on between two or more nations.

pastime: an activity that someone does regularly for enjoyment rather than work.

perfect game: a game in which a pitcher (or combination of pitchers) pitches a victory in which no opposing player reaches base.

pinch hitter: a pinch hitter is a substitute batter. Batters can be substituted at any time while the ball is dead.

pitcher's mound: the low, artificial hill where the pitcher stands when throwing a pitch.

run batted in (RBI): a statistic used in baseball and softball to credit a batter when the outcome of his or her at bat results in a run being scored.

sandlot: a piece of unoccupied land used by children for games.

tagging up: a baserunner "tags up" when he/she retouches or remains on their starting base until either the ball lands in fair territory or is touched by a fielder.